MISSION: Building a Super Fantastic World!

This book belongs to:

I would like to thank Lynn M., Jacob M., Roxanna K., and Bill M.,

who helped me create this amazing book.

You are awesome!

Haneul, Bill, Angela and Roxanna are in grade six at Peace Junior Elementary School and are part of a leadership club at their school. The students in this club are responsible for observing and talking with other students during recess and to help them find solutions to their problems.

They meet weekly and during their meeting they discuss all the information they have gathered.

Last week, they learned that there are some students who bully others on the playground, which is unacceptable! So, they decided to look into ways to stop bullying in their school.

During their discussion, Bill explained that bullying could be defined as the set of behaviours, gestures, or rude words that some students may use to isolate others. He added that there is another type of bullying, called "cyber-bullying".

No to cyber-bullying!!!

    All grade six students need to be educated on this topic because next school year they will be going to grade seven at a different school.
    Bill explains that cyber-bullying is a type of bullying that can occur through social media. For example, using the Internet, a student can send a hurtful message to another student in their school. Angela responds that this is a good idea and that all grade six students in their school should get more information about cyber-bullying behaviour and that it will help them protect themselves from this type of bullying.

Roxanna says that bullying and cyber-bullying have consequences. A student who is often bullied by another student may feel isolated and sometimes afraid to come to school. This student may feel bad about himself or herself and lose self-esteem or confidence. As a result, the student who does cyber-bullying should be given a serious warning or suspension for making the other person feel bad.

Haneul added that bullying and cyber-bullying should not be tolerated and should stop in every school in the world.

Roxanna also noted that there are so many other issues in school that should be discussed by student leaders. We need to think about creating better schools and a better world.

The four friends thought it would be a good idea to brainstorm a project to change some of the inappropriate behaviours in schools. They began to develop the idea of changing schools starting with their own. Angela says that students are the future citizens of the world. So, it is up to them to develop ideas to change all the schools in the world! This will help make the world a better place, which is a great mission!

One Saturday, they met at Angela's house to do research and discuss what they could include in their project to change their school and other schools around the world. After a few hours, they agreed on important points such as respect, peace, inclusion, social justice, quality education for all, etc.

After their research, Roxanna, Haneul, Angela, and Bill decided to illustrate their project so that they could easily make presentations to the entire school. They decided to persuade other students to join them in their mission to change the world.

They want to create a safer environment for all students to feel secure in their ability to learn.

A few days later, they showed their project to their teacher who congratulated them and helped them correct some grammar mistakes. With the approval of their teacher and the school administration, they organized a big assembly at the school. The gym room was full as there were many students and teachers. They also invited two local journalists because they anticipated that their speech would be one of the biggest speeches of their lives. The four friends had their notes and posters in their hands.

Here are their presentations:

Roxanna Liu's presentation:

Ladies, gentlemen, and fellow students,

Hello,

My name is Roxanna Liu and I am a grade six student. I am part of the student leadership club at our Peace Junior Public School. We are a group of four students (Haneul, Angela, Bill and myself) who are on a mission to change our school and other schools in the world.

Some of you may be wondering why we want to follow this mission and how we are going to fulfill it. Well, we conducted our little investigation by talking to several students during recess, which gave us a lot of information.

Over the past few days, we have been researching various issues in our school and elsewhere, and today each of us would like to share our vision. I invite you to follow along and listen carefully.

Let us think for a moment about the children of all the schools in the world, that is to say, of all the continents: Europe, America, Asia, Africa and Oceania.

We can see that they all have different skin colours. The world belongs to all of us. All of our beautiful skin colours look like a garden of flowers shining on the Earth. It is extraordinary, isn't it? This beauty of colours should not divide us, but rather unite us.

We must learn to respect each other by respecting each others' cultures. We must be kind to each other and our schools must be places of learning where there is peace, not discrimination and violence. Why am I talking about discrimination and violence? It is because we have gathered information that during lunch time, some students single out others because their meals are different from what they are used to seeing and these singled out students feel excluded and alone. Also, during recess, some students hit others for no reason or because they do not want to play with them.

No discrimination!

No to bullying and no to discrimination!

I invite you to join us in standing up against discrimination and violence. Let's say yes to peace, respect, and kindness to create a better and super fantastic world!

Haneul Lee's presentation:

Hello,

   My name is Haneul Lee and I have been working on this project with Angela, Roxanna, and Bill, and here is what we have discovered. As we have been interviewing students at our school over the past few weeks and doing our research, we have realized that there is a lot of bullying going on, not only in this school, but in many other schools as well. However, bullying, cyber-bullying, violence, and discrimination cannot help us build a better world!

One day, a student told us that if the planet Mars was habitable, that he would rather go live there because he thinks that on Mars there would be no bullying. Can you believe that?

So, we invite you to think about this question. Don't you think bullying is bad? If so, what should we do to stop bullying in our schools?

We want schools where every student feels safe and is not afraid of being bullied by others.

We realized that when a group of students play outside at recess, they only play with their best friends. We have often seen students who are alone because they don't have friends or because others don't want to include them. Don't you think it would be better to include others in your games, especially students who are alone?

Let's say yes to kindness!

   Imagine if we were kind to each other, our world would become a great place! With our will and a little effort, it is possible to create an extraordinary world.

We must first learn to respect ourselves and to be disciplined. Let's always try to do good things, even if no one sees us, and always be honest. Let's always make good decisions, and with this vision, we can create a great world. Join us in saying no to bullying and cyber-bullying. Let's say yes to honesty, integrity, inclusion, and create a great world!

Angela Robins' presentation:

Hello,

My name is Angela Robins, and I worked on this project with Roxanna, Bill and Haneul. While doing our research, we realized that as children, we have rights. For example, every child in any country should have the right to go to school. In order to succeed, every child must have a quality education.

Let me explain what a quality education is. It is an education that allows each student to be supported in his or her studies so that he or she can better succeed in life.

    Quality education is also about having beautiful schools, and airy, well-equipped classrooms that have laptops so students can better complete their research projects. Schools also need well-equipped libraries and supportive teachers to ensure that students receive a quality education.

This quality education can enable students to excel not only in Math and Science, but also in understanding our world. We would like to suggest that there can be frequent debates in schools for students to discuss issues related to social justice and equity. This will teach them to think critically and become well-informed global citizens.

Our mission is to create a world where every child has access to a quality education no matter where he/she lives.

We want a world without social injustice and inequality; a world that will produce millions of well-informed future citizens in every country. Join us in saying yes to quality education for all, social justice, and equity for all.

Bill Ishimwe's presentation:

Hello,

My name is Bill Ishimwe. As Roxanna said, we are students who want schools to be places of equal opportunity for all. You may ask why, but the answer is simple: It is simply because as young people we need to prepare ourselves to be good citizens, well-informed and well prepared for our future jobs. All students can succeed with the help of the school, and to do this, schools can set up tutoring clubs or after-school activities for students who need them.

In the tutoring clubs, there may be courses like Mathematics, Science, Languages (French, English or others), Music and Sports, etc. Such activities can help students improve in different areas. This equal opportunity could help every student succeed without any problem.

Let us be young leaders who can help our schools and the world become a magical world, a world filled with honey, cake, beautiful smiles, kindness, cooperation, honesty, integrity, discipline, etc.

Let's work together! Let's say yes to cooperation!

Let's share!

We must create a world where peace flows like a river that never stops. A world without violence, without discrimination, without cyber-bullying. Imagine that world! Who would like to live in such a world?

It is not tomorrow, not the day after tomorrow, but it is now, it is today, that we must take the first step to change our world and make it a better place!

After Bill, Angela, Roxanna, and Haneul's presentations, all the students in the gym room started clapping and saying, "Yes, yes, we want a super fantastic world, we want a super fantastic world."

The two journalists in the auditorium took many pictures of their presentations. They also wrote about their great mission to change the world.

A few days later, Angela, Roxanna, Bill and Haneul were invited to different TV shows to explain their extraordinary mission.

Today, Angela, Roxanna, Bill and Haneul invite you to help them in their mission to build a better and super fantastic world together.

Do you think Angela, Roxanna, Bill and Haneul have a good mission? Why or why not? What other important points might you suggest they include in their presentations or mission? Explain your answer!

What can you do to make this world a better place?

Mission: Building a Super Fantastic World!

Written by Eugénie Mujawiyera
Illustrated by Chris Rutayisire

Copyright©2023 by Eugénie Mujawiyera

(Eugeniebooks15@gmail.com)

Other books written by Eugénie Mujawiyera:

-READING: An Incredible Wealth!
-HAVING BIG DREAMS! What does it take to become...!

All rights reserved

www.ingramcontent.com/pod-product-compliance
Lightning Source LLC
Chambersburg PA
CBHW042029100526
44587CB00029B/4350